Jake arrives at Euston station in London. It is a holiday weekend and it is his first time away from Manchester. Jake is eighteen years old and he lives with his family. Now he is in London. He is very happy. He stops and looks at his map.

'I can go to the Notting Hill Carnival and I can see some interesting places from the bus too,' he thinks.

Jake is sitting on a red London bus behind a big family.
The children are standing at the windows. They are
looking for famous places.

'Look! There's Madame Tussaud's! Can we go there?'

'Not today,' their mother answers. 'We're going to the
carnival.'

'They're going to Notting Hill too,' Jake thinks.

It is a hot afternoon and Jake is sitting on a bench in
Notting Hill. Suddenly, he sees some people in costumes.
They have balloons and drums in their hands.

'Does the carnival start here?' Jake asks Mel, a girl in a
green dress.

'Yes, near here. Look at the floats!' she says. 'Listen to
the music! The procession is starting.'

Suddenly, a tall girl runs to the first float. Her costume is yellow and red and she has feathers in her hair. The young men on the float shout to her.

'Quickly, Maria! You're late!'

'Sorry – a little problem with my job,' she says. 'But it's OK now.'

The band moves slowly down the street.

Jake looks at the beautiful tall girl in her carnival
costume. Their eyes meet and she smiles at him.
Suddenly, he knows. It's love!
Jake's new friends are standing and waiting for him. But
he walks away from them. He can only see Maria. Mel
talks to Jake but he doesn't hear her. She looks at Maria
and she understands.

The carnival procession moves down the street. On the
floats people are dancing to the music. Some people in
the street are dancing too. There is a lot of music, noise
and colour.

Jake is running but there are crowds of people near him.
He can't stay with Maria's float. How can he meet this
beautiful girl? Who is she?

Maria looks down and sees Jake again. He has a friendly face and she likes him too.

'I'm Jake. What's your name?' he shouts.

'Hi, Jake! I'm Maria,' she answers.

'Can I telephone you? What's your number?'

She gives a big smile. But Jake can't hear her! The band is playing and people are shouting.

The procession goes near a street café. People are
drinking coffee at tables on the street. A tourist is
standing on a chair. He is making a film of the carnival.
His wife is watching him.

Jake sees a camera on the table. He wants a photograph of
Maria. He takes the camera and runs quickly after the float.
'Maria! Maria! I want a photo! Smile, please!'

The procession is moving slowly. There are crowds of
people in the street and Jake can't see Maria now.
'I can run down a quiet street and find her float,' he thinks.
He tries the first street. Suddenly, he hears the music
from the band. He is near the procession now.
He sees Maria's float and shouts, 'Maria! I'm here!'
She sees him and she waves.

The tourist finds a policeman.

'A young man in a red T-shirt – he has my camera!' he says.

'Yes, I understand. Can you see him now?'

'It's very difficult in this crowd. But wait . . . yes, I can see him! There he is!'

Jake is standing on a bench.

'Look! That's him and that's my camera!'

Jake puts his photograph of Maria in his pocket. He is happy now. The policeman and the tourist run to him.

'Come down, young man,' the policeman says. 'Is that your camera?'

'No, it's *my* camera,' the man says.

Jake's face is red. Now he has a problem.

'Sorry, I only want one photo. Here's your camera.'

'I'm very sorry,' Jake says. 'I never do this.'

Jake thinks of his mother and he is very unhappy. The tourists think of their son and suddenly they are unhappy too.

'We have our camera now,' they say. 'He isn't a bad boy. Please, can he go?'

'No, I can't do that,' the policeman says.

Jake is standing in front of a police sergeant.

'Now, in your pockets you have . . . a map, a pen, £5.73, a train ticket. Is that all?'

'Let's see this important photo,' the first policeman says.

Jake takes the photo from his back pocket and gives it to the sergeant. The sergeant looks at the photograph for a long time. He is surprised.

'Where's Policewoman Day?' the sergeant asks.

'She's at the doctor's,' a policewoman says.

'No, she's here again now,' a policeman says. 'Do you want her?'

'Yes. Send her in. We have a problem.'

The policeman walks to the door and says, 'Please come in, Policewoman Day.'

The policemen look at the photo and they smile. Why?
Jake doesn't understand.

The door opens and Policewoman Day comes in. She
looks at Jake. He looks at her. They are very surprised.

'It's you!' they say at the same time.

'Look at this photo, Maria,' the sergeant says. 'Here you
are at the doctor's – or perhaps the carnival?'

ACTIVITIES

Before you read

1   Find these words in your dictionary. They are all in the story. What are they in your language?

   balloon   band   bench   camera   carnival   costume   crowd

   drum   feather   float (n)   *map   pocket   procession   sergeant*

   shout   surprised   T-shirt   tourist   wave (v)   *wife*

2   Do you have carnivals in your country? When? What do people do?

After you read

3   Answer the questions.
   a   What is Maria's job?
   b   Why does Jake take a tourist's camera?
   c   The tourist doesn't see Jake. Why not?
   d   Why is the sergeant surprised at Jake's photo?
   e   Why is Jake surprised in the police station?

4   Work with a friend.
   Student A: You are the sergeant. Ask questions about Jake and
                  about the camera.
   Student B: You are Jake. Answer the sergeant's questions.

5   It is the day after the carnival. Write a letter from Jake, in London, to his mother.